W9-BTA-074

To: _____

From: _____

Other books by Gregory E. Lang:

Why a Daughter Needs a Mom

Why a Son Needs a Dad

Why a Son Needs a Mom

Why I Love Grandma

Why I Love Grandpa

Why I Chose You

Why I Love You

Why I Still Love You

Why I Need You

Why We Are a Family

Why We Are Friends

Brothers and Sisters

Simple Acts

Love Signs

Life Maps

Thank You, Mom

Thank You, Dad

Why a Daughter Needs a Dad

· 100 Reasons ·

GREGORY E. LANG

WITH PHOTOGRAPHS BY JANET LANKFORD–MORAN

CUMBERLAND HOUSE

AN IMPRINT OF SOURCEBOOKS, INC.®

Published by Cumberland House Publishing, an imprint of Sourcebooks, Inc.
P.O. Box 4410, Naperville, Illinois 60567–4410
(630) 961–3900
Fax: (630) 961–2168
www.sourcebooks.com

Printed and bound in China

OGP   20 19 18 17 16 15 14 13 12 11

To Meagan, the inspiration for what
I do right, the reason I try to do no wrong.
—DAD

For my dad, who fostered creativity, and Helen,
who gave guidance at just the right time.
—JANET

INTRODUCTION

I was born into a loving family. My family is the kind that embraces you, nurtures you, and loves you immeasurably. For me the most anticipated event of the year is our reunion at Thanksgiving, a tradition with a thirty-year history. I look forward to the sound of cheerful greetings, the warmth of hugs and firm handshakes, the comfort of kisses and familiar smells, and the retelling of stories of a Thanksgiving past, all of which rush toward me as soon as I set foot inside the front door. This love I have received shapes the love I give, and I hope it is evident at its best in my relationship with my daughter.

I have known from an early age that I wanted to be a father, and particularly the father of a daughter. My heart always melted when I held a baby girl, and I grew envious when I watched a toddler crawl onto her dad's lap to cuddle. I've been touched by women who spoke fondly of their fathers and moved by the grief of women who have lost their fathers. The special love shared between a daughter and father was something I very much wanted to experience for myself.

When my wife told me she was pregnant I was overjoyed. Something inside me told me that our child would be a girl. Throughout the pregnancy I referred to the baby as "she"—never "it"—and when we saw the first sonogram I insisted that it was obviously a girl, even though the doctor said it was too early to tell. I was in the delivery room when she arrived. The first person she looked at was me. I was smitten instantly.

After the delivery an exhausted mother slept while Meagan Katherine and I bonded. She slept on my shoulder, her face nestled under my chin. We spent her first night in the world together, asleep in a big recliner. Today, nearly twelve years later, Meagan still lays her head on my shoulder and turns her face into my neck. I still pull her close and make sure no harm comes to her.

Over the years Meagan and I have shared many special times together. We've had daddy-daughter dates, traveled, explored new subjects, and done sweet things for one another now and then. Sometimes we sit on the floor and look through the contents of the "Meagan Box," a cardboard box overstuffed with pictures, her art-work, keepsakes, and notes we have written to each other. In that box resides the reassuring evidence of our close relationship. Her mother and I divorced years ago, and Meagan lives with me half time. During the weeks that she is with her mother, I go to that box often. For a long time I have wanted to capture those memories and put them together in some form to give to Meagan, to reassure her that when we are not together I think of her and I love her.

I knew from the start that my relationship with Meagan would be a changing one. I knew, and people told me, that one day she would be a little less affectionate, more interested in friends, and less entertained by me, and that she might even find me embarrassing. It has surely come to pass. Now when I take her to school, she kisses me good-bye, and never on the lips, *before* we leave the house. I must turn off my music the moment the car enters school territory. I am to keep both hands on the wheel, my gaze fixed straight ahead. I may wave at other parents, but only if they wave first. If I must say, "I love you," it is to be nearly whispered, and never if the car door is open. Sometimes I go to the Meagan Box to reassure myself.

When I first began this book my intention was to create a different kind of how-to book, a book daughters could give to their fathers to tell them what they wanted from them. I sat and thought about what my daughter and I had done together. I thought about what kinds of experiences my father had shared with my sister, and my uncles with my cousins. I asked Meagan for ideas, and I turned to the book of Proverbs for inspiration. Then I wrote it all down. The first time I read what I had written I saw a list of what a daughter might ask her father to do for her (just as I had planned). The second time I read it I saw a list of all that I hope to do for my daughter. The third time I read it I saw myself telling Meagan that she would change but never outgrow me. When I read it the fourth time, I knew I was holding the Meagan Box.

Happy with the text, I set out to find a photographer. I did not know Janet Lankford-Moran when I began this book. I literally picked her at random out of the newspaper where she appeared in an article about a local art college. I sent her my manuscript and asked her to work with me. We met one afternoon to talk business. During this meeting she told me her personal story. She was raised by her single father beginning in her early childhood. She shared with me that she could see herself and her father in much of the manuscript. I knew then that we had to complete this book together. I did not have to tell Janet what I wanted the photographs to convey. She knew herself, perhaps even better than I.

With this book Janet and I hope to inspire new as well as experienced fathers to embrace the challenging role they play in their daughters' lives, to give them the love, nurture, and support they seek, and to cherish that which is reciprocated in kind. With this book I tell my child how very irreplaceably important she is to me. With this book I comfort and reassure myself that I will always have the pleasure and honor of being in her life. I love you, Meagan Katherine.

WHY A DAUGHTER NEEDS A DAD

A daughter needs a dad

to learn that when he says it will

be okay soon, it will.

A daughter needs a dad

who will make sacrifices

so she will not have to sacrifice.

A daughter needs a dad . . .

who will laugh at her at all the right times.

to teach her that her value as a person is more than the way she looks.

who will not punish her for her mistakes,

but help her learn from them.

A daughter needs a dad . . .

who will always have time to give her

hugs and kisses.

who does not mind when she steps

on his shoes while dancing.

who will always make sure

she has a place to come home to.

A daughter needs a dad

who will never think she is
too old to need him.

A daughter needs a dad . . .

to teach her to believe

that she deserves to be treated well.

to teach her to accept the differences in others.

to teach her to weigh the consequences

of her actions and make decisions accordingly.

A daughter needs a dad

to make the family whole and complete.

■   ■   ■   ■   ■   ■   ■

A daughter needs a dad . . .

to protect her from scary nighttime creatures.

to answer the questions that keep her awake at night.

to protect her from thunder and lightning.

A daughter needs a dad

so she will know what it is like
to be somebody's favorite.

A daughter needs a dad . . .

to make the complex simple and the painful bearable.

to tell her that all is not hopeless, even when she feels it is.

to join her journey when she is too afraid
to walk alone.

to teach her the meaning of integrity,
and how to avoid the crooked path.

A daughter needs a dad

to tell her truthfully

that she is the most beautiful of all.

A daughter needs a dad . . .

to make the tough decisions for her

until she is able to make them for herself.

to teach her that forgiving is a natural thing to do.

to teach her that she can forgive more than once.

A daughter needs a dad

to teach her that family
is more important than work.

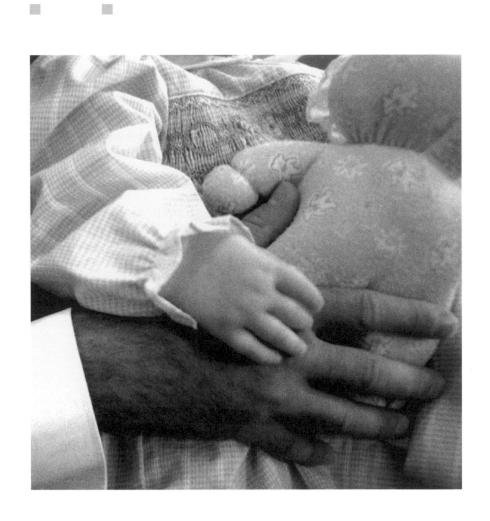

A daughter needs a dad

to be the safe spot she can always turn to.

A daughter needs a dad

to show her how it feels to be loved unselfishly.

A daughter needs a dad

to be the standard against which
she will judge all men.

A daughter needs a dad . . .

to teach her the difference between

being firm and being stubborn.

to teach her that she is equal
to her husband.

to teach her that respect is to be earned,

as he has earned hers.

A daughter needs a dad . . .

to learn what she should expect from her husband.

to teach her how to be responsible for others.

to teach her to preserve her dignity
during difficult times.

to help her believe in herself as a parent,
and that in discipline there is hope.

A daughter needs a dad

who will influence her life even when he isn't with her.

A daughter needs a dad

so that she will have at least one hero
who will not let her down.

A daughter needs a dad

to tuck her in at night.

A daughter needs a dad

to protect her when she is not wise enough
to protect herself.

A daughter needs a dad . . .

to teach her to be honest in all her dealings.

to teach her patience and kindness.

to teach her when to be firm and when to compromise.

to help her try again whenever she fails.

A daughter needs a dad

to help her take the risks
that will build her confidence.

A daughter needs a dad

to prepare her to persevere through hardship.

A daughter needs a dad

who will let her know that while she
may not be the center of someone else's world,
she is the center of his.

A daughter needs a dad . . .

to give her the guidance she needs

as she begins to resolve her own troubles.

to pull her back when she is headed in the wrong direction.

to think highly of her when no one else will.

to hold her as she cries.

A daughter needs a dad

to be the history of her family
for her own children.

A daughter needs a dad

to teach her what it means
to always be there.

A daughter needs a dad

to teach her that a man's strength
is not the force of his hand or his voice,
but the kindness of his heart.

A daughter needs a dad . . .

to teach her to recognize truth and reward it.

to teach her to recognize sincerity and encourage it.

to teach her about fairness.

to teach her to stand up for herself.

A daughter needs a dad

to remind her of what she may not remember.

■　■　■　■　■　■　■

A daughter needs a dad

to give her the gentle pushes
that help her grow.

A daughter needs a dad

so that when no one else is there for her,

she can close her eyes and see him.

A daughter needs a dad

to carry her just because she wants to be carried.

A daughter needs a dad

to set a moral standard for her.

A daughter needs a dad

to share with her the wisdom
she has not yet acquired.

A daughter needs a dad . . .

to calm her when she is stressed by her challenges.

who teaches her she is important by stopping what he is doing to watch her.

to give her a strong, willful character.

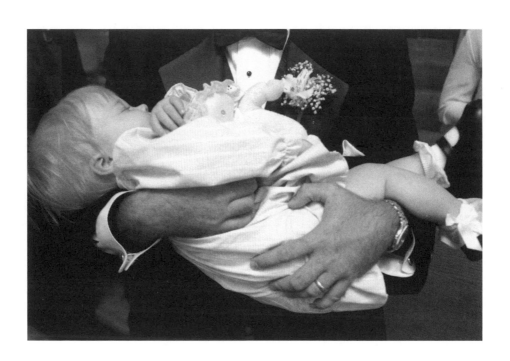

A daughter needs a dad

to remind her of the comfort
of being held near and feeling secure.

A daughter needs a dad

to build a loving house on a foundation
of wisdom and understanding.

A daughter needs a dad . . .

to help around the house so that her mother
will have time to spend with her, too.

to teach her that her role in a family is greater than
the work she does.

to help her become the best mother she can be.

A daughter needs a dad . . .

to teach her how things work.

*to show her how to fix things
for herself.*

to fix her favorite things.

A daughter needs a dad

to teach her the importance of being a lady.

A daughter needs a dad

who gives her refuge
in a home secured with faith.

A daughter needs a dad . . .

to teach her that ignorance is not an excuse for anything.

to teach her not to let pride
get in the way of discovering new things.

to teach her to experiment
for the sake of testing her own assumptions.

to teach her how to focus her mind
in the midst of distraction.

A daughter needs a dad

to teach her the joy of serving others.

A daughter needs a dad

to show her that true love is unconditional.

A daughter needs a dad . . .

to tell her all she needs to know about boys.

to show her that all boys

are not like the one who hurt her.

to teach her how to recognize a gentleman.

A daughter needs a dad

to teach her that loving her family is a priority.

A daughter needs a dad

to teach her that a joyful heart is filled
with peace rather than deceit.

A daughter needs a dad

to teach her when to be cautious.

A daughter needs a dad

to teach her that men and women can be good friends.

A daughter needs a dad . . .

to teach her what kind of man to choose

to be the father of her children.

to stand with her on the day she marries

the man she hopes will be just like her father.

to help her raise her children with strong family values.

A daughter needs a dad

to teach her to learn from her experiences.

■   ■   ■   ■   ■   ■   ■

A daughter needs a dad

to help her find her way in life.

A daughter needs a dad . . .

to show her the benefits of hard work.

to teach her to spend responsibly,

save for a rainy day,

and give with a generous heart.

to help her finish her work when she is too weary to finish it herself.

A daughter needs a dad

so she learns that men can be trustworthy.

A daughter needs a dad

because without him she will have
less in her life than she deserves.

To Contact the Author or Photographer

write in care of the publisher:
Cumberland House Publishing/Sourcebooks, Inc.
P.O. Box 4410
Naperville, IL 60567-4410

email the author or visit his Web site:
greg.lang@mindspring.com
www.gregoryelang.com

email the photographer or visit her Web site:
janet@oijoyphoto.com
www.oijoyphoto.com